Things That Go "TAT" In The Night

This book is dedicated to you, the reader.
I hope that you enjoy this collection of fun patterns.

All rights reserved. You may tat as many of the items from these patterns as you wish, and may sell your tatted items or give them away. You may NOT copy, modify, or distribute these patterns in any way without prior written permission of the author.

Copyright © 2006 Ruth Perry - Rozella Linden Tatting
First Printing 2006
Linden Publishing

Revised Edition 2014
Copyright © 2014 Ruth Perry - Rozella Linden Tatting
ISBN-13: 978-1500586089
ISBN-10: 1500586080

Table of Contents

Black Widow Spider	2
Small Spider & A Fly	9
Celtic Knot Pumpkin	10
Celtic Knot Owl	11
Celtic Knot Bat	13
Baby Bat	19
BDS Balanced Double Stitch	22
Beaded Double Core Reversed Ring	26

Terms & Notation

DS	Tatting stitch or double stitch
-	Picot
+ or Join	Join to a previously tatted picot.
Ring (2 – 2)	Tat a ring with 2ds, a picot, then 2ds, and then close the ring.
turn	Reverse work or flip it over top to bottom
CTM	Continuous Thread Method – do not cut the thread between the ball and shuttle.
Chain ##	Tat a chain of ## DS. ## indicates the number of DS to tat.

Black Widow Spider

This spider is tatted with red for the hourglass and black for the spider. She is a three-dimensional Celtic tatted spider with wire in the eight legs.

Begin with size 10 or 20 red thread. Wind about half a yard of thread on the shuttle, CTM, without cutting from the ball of thread. (**C**ontinuous **T**hread **M**ethod)

Tie a knot in the thread between the shuttle and the ball. Make your first DS about a picot's distance from the knot forming a picot at the beginning of the chain.

Chain - 10 - 10 - 10

Weave the Cletic Trefoil knot, and then tie the ends in a square knot through the beginning picot.

Chain 10 - 10 - 10

Weave the Cletic Trefoil knot, and then tie the ends at the beginning picot. Hide the ends. Cut close to the work.

Weave the Trefoil Knot	Join at Picot	Completed Hourglass

Abdomen (black thread)

Ring 1 (3 - 3 + 3 - 3) turn, Join to Picot A of hourglass - see photo

Chain 12 turn

Ring 2 (3 - 6 - 3) turn

Chain 12 turn

Ring 3 (3 - 3 + 3 - 3) turn, Join to Picot B of hourglass - see photo

Chain 12 turn

Ring 4 (3 - 3 + 3 - 3) turn, Join to Picot C of hourglass - see photo

Chain 12 turn

Ring 5 (3 - 6 - 3) turn

Chain 12 turn

In this photo the 6th ring has not been tatted yet.

After tatting the 6th ring this piece will no longer lie flat, but will form a bowl shape.

The sixth ring joins to the final picot " D " of the hourglass and to the first picot of the first ring.

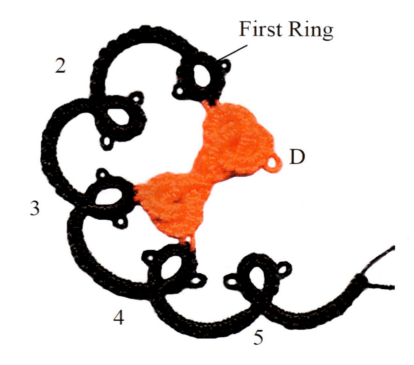

Ring 6 (3 - 3 + 3 + 3) turn, Join to Picot D of hourglass and picot of 1st ring

Chain 12 turn, Pull up to weave through 1st row chain

Ring 7 (3 + 6 + 3) turn, Join to picot of 1st ring and 2nd ring

Chain 12 turn, Pull up to weave through 1st row chain

Ring 8 (3 + 6 + 3) turn, Join to picot of 2nd ring and 3rd ring

Chain 8 - 4 turn. Pull up to weave through 1st row chain

Ring 9 (3 + 6 + 3) turn, Join to picot of 3rd ring and 4th ring

Chain 4 - 8 turn, Pull up to weave through 1st row chain

Ring 10 (3 + 6 + 3) turn, Join to picot of 4th ring and 5th ring

Chain 12 turn, Pull up to weave through 1st row chain

Ring 11 (3 + 6 + 3) turn, Join to picot of 5th ring and 6th ring

Chain 12 turn, Pull up to weave through 1st row chain,

Tie ends around base of 1st ring. THC

Eighth Ring

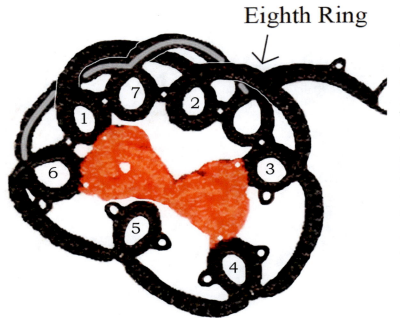

The photo at the left shows the eighth ring completed and the following chain with a picot for joining to the Spider body.

Notice that the chain needs to be pulled up through to weave it over the chain from the first round. Just use a hook to pull it up through. The grey lines show the previous second round chains already woven through.

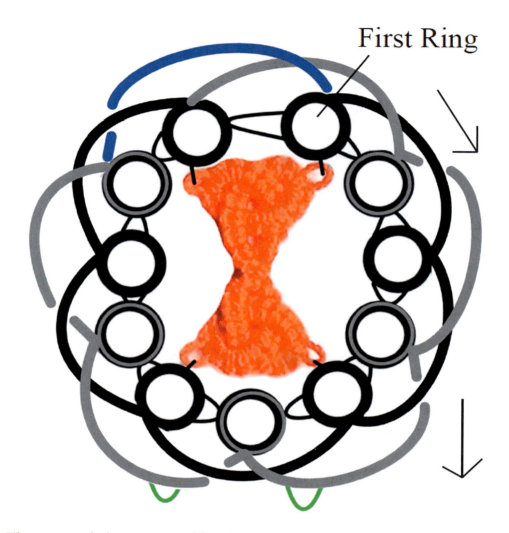

The second time around is shown above, but flatened. The rings and chains in the first row are black, and the rings and chains in the second row are grey. The final chain is shown in blue. It is tied to the base of the very first ring, then hide the ends and cut. The chains are all 12 DS except for where the abdomen of the spider is joined to the thorax by the two picots on the chains shown in green.

Notice that the second time around the chains weave under and over the chains from the first round. Make sure that the weaving is correct before tatting the next ring.

It is easier to tat this part with needle tatting, finger tatting, or using a celtic shuttle, or even a shuttle with a bobbin that is easy to unwind then wind again each time to weave through.

Spider Body, Head, and Legs

The Legs can be tatted anytime before beginning the body, so if you want to tat lots of legs for many spiders ahead of time, you may do so.

Begin with four pieces of black wire about twice the length desired for each leg plus 1/4 to 1/2 inch for the rings at each end that are formed using jewlry pliers the same way you would make a jump ring. The size of the wire and length will depend upon the size thread you are using for the spider so it looks right proportionally.

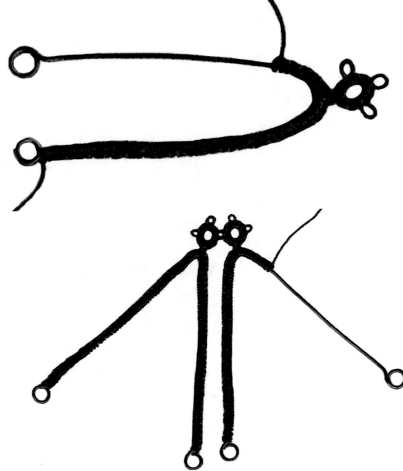

Place the tatted ring at the center of the wire, then tat over the wire to the proper length for each leg. Tie, hide, and cut the ends. Tatting over the piece of wire can be done as direct tatting with a shuttle or if the wire is sturdy enough, just tat over it as if needle tatting, but tighten each stitch snug against the previous stitch.

Legs (black thread)

Leg1 & 2 Ring (3 - 3 - 3 - 3)

Tat over wire for both legs

Leg3 & 4 Ring (3 - 3 - 3 + 3) Join to Picot of ring for legs 1 & 2

Tat over wire for both legs.

Make another set of legs the same way for the other four spider legs

Body (black thread)

Center Ring:

Ring (2 + 2 + 2 - 2 + 2 + 2)
This joins to the center picot of each of the rings for the legs.

Split Ring (3 + 3 / 3 + 3) turn

Chain 3 + 3 Join to picot of the abdomen.

To go around the space between the ring and the legs, the ball thread goes under and the shuttle thread goes over.

Chain 3 Go around in the space between the ring and the first pair of legs.

Chain 3 Go around the space between the ring and the next pair of legs

Chain 6 turn

Ring (3 + 3 + 3 + 3) Join to the picots of the leg rings and the center

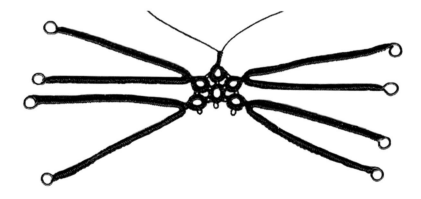

The photo above shows all eight legs completed, and joined to the center ring of the body. The split ring already tatted joins to the two sets of legs. The first three DS of the chain is completed, and ready to join to the abdomen.

Once joined to the abdomen, and the chains completed around the body which stabilize the position of the legs this piece is truly three dimensional.

Head:

Tat this ring with the ball thread (on a second shuttle or finger tatting)

Ring (5 - 5)

Fold this ring over so the picot touches the base of the ring, and then join through the picot and tie a square knot around the base of the ring to hold it in place.

Body Continued:

Chain 6

Chain 3 Go around the space between the ring and the next pair of legs.

Chain 3 Go around the space between the ring and the next pair of legs.

Chain 3 + 3 Join to the other picot of the abdomen.

Tie the ends to the base of the split ring. Hide the ends and cut close to the work.

Tatted Spider & A FLY !!!

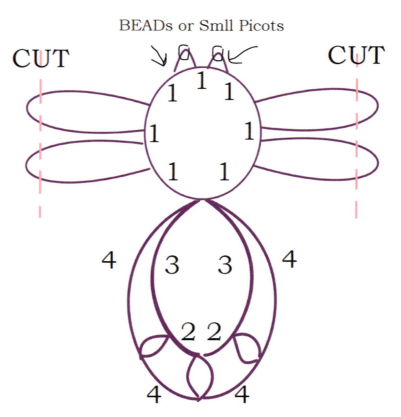

Beads are optional, so if using beads for the eyes thread two beads on the thread before winding about a yard on the shuttle. Leave a thread end about 1/2 yard then cut the thread from the ball.

Ring (1 VLP 1 VLP 1 SP 1 SP 1 VLP 1 VLP 1)
This is the thorax, head, eyes, and legs.

Ring (3 - 2 - 2 - 3)

Split Ring (6 + 4 / 6 + 4) Join to the picots of the previous ring.

Pull the carrying thread up through the center picot of the inside ring, and tie the thread ends in a square knot. The thread ends are the web the spider spins. Add a clear bead to the threads here if desired, and another thread to make twisted cord for a bookmark. You may use either beads or picots for the eyes.

Cut the leg picot ends as shown, or leave them for the wings of a tatted fly.
"Step into my parlor said the spider to the fly."

VLP is a Very Long Picot

This is an easy spider to tat for demonstrating in the fall. Kids love them!!! Tatted in gold they are a great Christmas Spider.

Use any thread, any color, and any size, with or without beads..

I like to tat them in size 10 with bright color thread and give them away to all the kids..

Tatted Celtic Knot Pumpkin

Materials:

Green and Orange tatting or crochet thread. Size 8 pearl cotton makes it about 1.5" across. Size 70 thread makes it about 1/2" when finished.

Stem:

Wind about half a yard of size 12 Pearl cotton on a shuttle. Tie an overhand knot in the thread to start.

Chain 4 turn

Leaves:

Tat a small clover

Ring 1 (6 - 3 - 3)

Ring 2 (3 + 3 - 3) Join to ring 1

Ring 3 (3 + 3 - 6) Join to ring 2

Tie, hide, cut the ends close to the work.

Pumpkin body:

Wind about a yard of size 8 orange pearl cotton thread on a shuttle CTM, do not cut from the ball.

Join the orange thread to the free picot of ring #1 of the clover, and tat a Chain of about 120 DS (enough to make 4 circles around when the stitches are pulled snug. Depending on your size of thread, more or less DS might look better. No matter, just 4 times around in a circle. This is lazy tatting… no specific number of DS to count. Large thread looks better with more DS (150), small thread looks better with fewer DS. Start weaving this knot in the center.

Weave the knot as shown on the next page.

And then the weaving continues up both sides of the knot. Weave the Celtic Knot as shown in the diagrams on the next page. When the knot is completed, tie the ends to the free picot on ring #3 of the clover, and then tat a short chain (about 10 DS) and then join back at the very beginning of the orange chain. This will help hold everything in place. Tie, hide the ends, and then cut close to the work.

The drawing here shows about 120 DS Tatted. Leave the thread ends about 12 to 15" long, and then cut from the ball and shuttle to make it easier to weave the knot. The green clover will weave through the knot with some care.

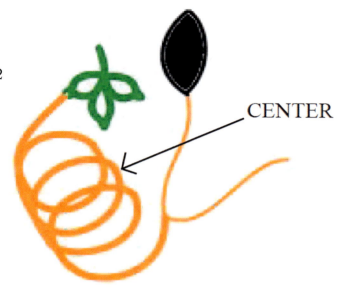

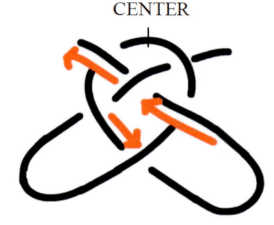

Begin Weaving the Celtic Knot at the center of the tatted chain. (this tatting must be fairly tight so that it curves into four circles.

Make a loop at the center by crossing the right side of the chain over the left. Then form a loop at the bottom left by placing the center loop over the chain as shown.

The loop on the bottom right is formed by weaving the chain over the center loop, then under the chain, then back over the center loop. Continue weaving the knot as shown.

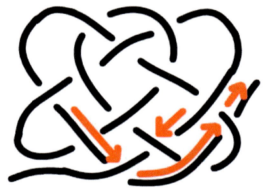

11

Celtic Knot Owl

Instructions:

Any size and color thread with about a yard wound on the shuttle CTM, do not cut from the ball.

Ring (3 eleven picots sep by 1 DS 3)
This is the first eye.

Chain 23 six picots 20 – 4 – 20 six picots 23
This is the body, wings and feet. These should be fairly tight so they curve quite a bit.

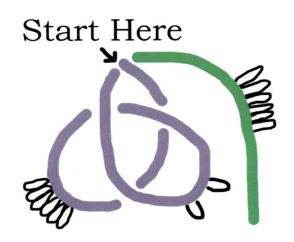
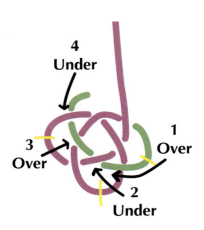

Weave Celtic Knot as shown. The eye is the end that weaves through the knot. Tie the threads in a square knot around the chain at the base of the eye to complete the Celtic Knot. Then tat the second eye.

Ring (3 eleven picots 3)
Next tie the thread ends in a square knot to hold the eyes in the proper place and cut the ball thread to about 6 in.

Ring (3 – 3)
This is the Beak. The end from the ball can be hidden in the beak ring while you tat. You may choose to use a bicone bead for the beak. Put the thread through the bead, through a seed bead, then back through the bicone bead.

Tighten the beak ring and pinch it so it looks like an owl beak. It will stick out in front of the eyes. Hide the shuttle thread end and cut.

Tatted Celtic Knot Bat

You will need wo shuttles wound CTM with any size and color thread.

This bat measures about eight inches wide when tatted with size 10 thread, and slightly smaller in size 20 thread. Size 80 thread makes about a four inch wing-span bat.

To tat long chains that will stay straight or curve in either direction, use the "Balanced Double Stitch" [BDS]. BChain is a chain of all BDS.

To tat the BDS, when you tat each half of the double stitch, go around the core thread two times instead of just once. This will give the chain stability and allow it to be shaped straight or curve in either direction.

Fig. 1	First Eye
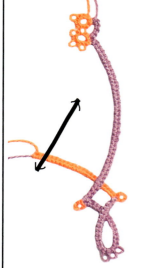 Tatted in two colors to show shuttle use, this piece is ready to be joined to the mouth picot. The weaving must be done before the join! When you join the Chain to the picot, shown by the arrow, the side of the body will curve out more so it will look like the finished bat photograph.	Shuttle #1 **Ring (3 – 3 – 3) turn** **BChain 5 turn** Mouth & Nose **Ring (2 + 2 – 2 – 2 – 2) turn** Body & legs **BChain 40 turn** **Ring (2 – 2) turn** **BChain 13 – 1 – 1 – 13 turn** **Ring (2 – 2) Do NOT Turn** Shuttle #2 **BChain (18 Weave the Chain over, then under, as shown + 18** **Do NOT Turn** You may adjust the 18 + 18 stitches to 21 + 21 if your tatting is very tight.

There are no joins in the legs and feet of the bat. The Bchains weave over and under; then you tat the Bchain that joins to the picot of the mouth. When you tat the second leg, it weaves over and under again for the second leg. Later, when the body of the bat is finished by weaving the Bchain between the wings through the body, it will hold the feet in place where they belong.

Be sure to shape the Bchains as you tat! This piece looks great when every Bchain is tatted to hold the shape it will have when the bat is finished. Some of the Bchains need to be fairly straight, others require quite a bit of curve. It will be stiff like tatted wire.

Figure Two

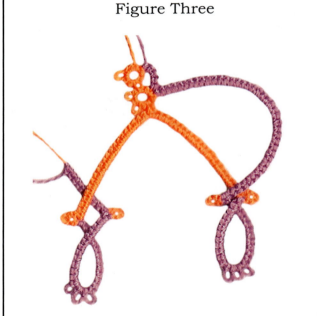

Shuttle #1

Ring (2 – 2) turn
Bchain (13 – 1 – 1 – 13) turn
Ring (2 – 2) turn
Bchain 40

Figure two shows the second leg tatted and the first 10 stitches of the Bchain 40. It is a good idea to stop and shape the tatting about every 10 stitches, snug them together, and straighten or curve them as they will be in the final piece. At this point, weave the Bchain over, then under, for the second leg.

Figure Three

Figure three shows the exact same tatting after weaving the Bchain for the second leg.

Continue tatting the remaining stitches of the 40 stitches for this Bchain section.

Join to the next picot of the mouth.

Bchain (5) turn

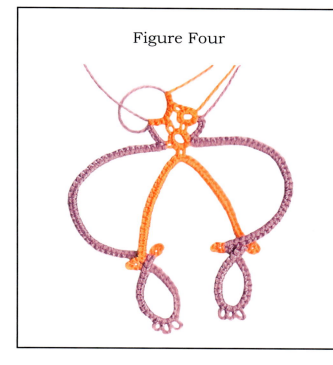

Figure Four

Second Eye

Ring (3 + 3 + 3) turn

There are several ways to put beads in the rings for the eyes. You may tat beaded double core reverse rings for beads that are actually tatted in the center of the rings, or any other method that you wish to use and feel comfortable doing.

Instructions for tatting Beaded Double Core Reverse Rings are at the end of this book.

Beads for the eyes are optional, but very attractive as you will see in the following photos.

Rounded Ears

Bchain 21 Join to the picot where the two eyes join together.

Chain 2 then join back into that same picot as the previous join.

Bchain 21 Join to the thread space at the base of the ring that forms the first eye.

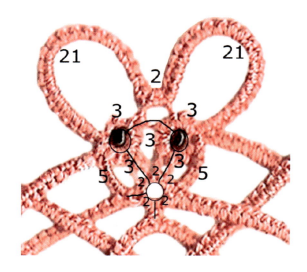

Wing 1

Shuttle #1
BChain 60 turn

Ring (2 – 2)

BChain 110

Shuttle #2
Ring (2 – 2) turn

BChain 35

Shuttle #1
Ring (2 – 2)

Weave this wing as shown.

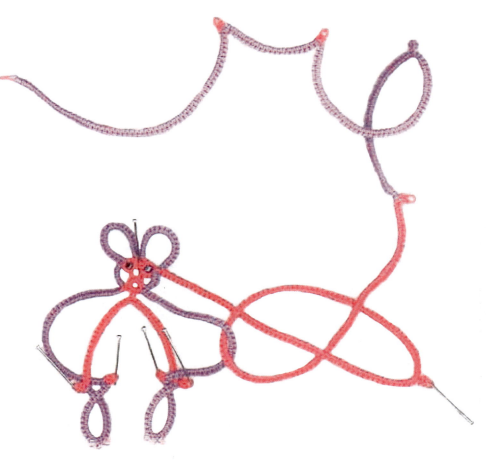

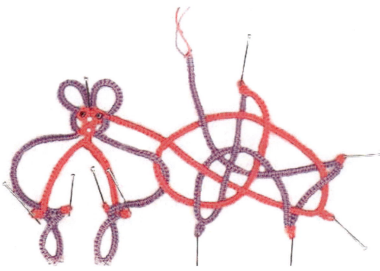

Pin the Bchain sections and rings for the wing in place onto a pillow or cutting mat and weave the wing by following these photos and the diagram.

Quilter's T pins work best. Pin through the picots of the small rings as you go.

This photo of the test tat bat by Katie Verna shows the first weave for the first wing.

Note: When you finish the tatting for the second wing, leave the ends long enough to easily tie to the head when you finish weaving the Celtic knot for the wing.

The ends of the thread appear to be short in this photo so that it is easier to see the BChains and the Celtic Knot wing.

Inside Body

Bchain 50 turn
Ring 2 - 2 turn
Bchain 50 turn

Weave the inside body through as shown.

Note: You do not have to unwind the shuttles to weave through the legs of the bat. Start the shuttle through in the correct manner, and then open up enough space to pass the shuttle through. When the shuttle is through the space, just twist the legs back the way they were.

Wing 2

Shuttle #2

BChain 60 turn
Ring (2 – 2) turn
BChain 21 turn
Ring (2 – 2) turn
BChain 50 turn
Ring (2 – 2)
BChain 35
Ring (2 – 2)
BChain 110
Ring (2 – 2)
BChain 60

Weave the second wing by flipping the bat over so the second wing is on the right side. Set up the BChains as shown by pinning them in place, and then weave the final BChain through as shown by the black arrows.

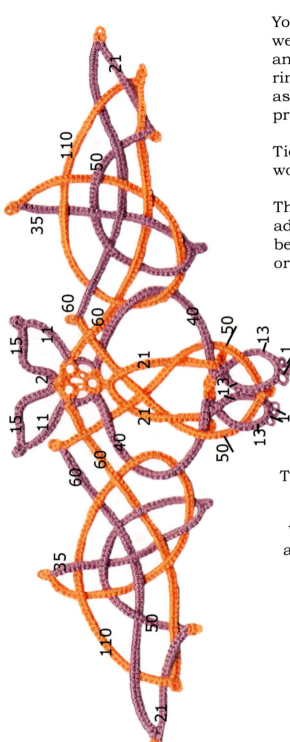

You must check to be certain that every weave over & under is done correctly, and then tie the ends to the base of the ring for the eye where the ear is attached as shown where the arrow points on the previous page.

Tie, Hide, Cut the ends close to the work.

The bat wings can be posed in flight. By adjusting the Celtic knot, the wings may be raised or lowered if he is to be sewn or glued onto a background or fabric.

This two color photo diagram shows the stitch counts and pointed ears.

When the bat is tatted in two colors it actually turns out to look like this one.

Two colors make it look awesome!

Baby Bat

Begin with a bead that is the right size to fit inside a tatted ring with 20 DS. Put the bead on the thread and then wind several yards of thread on a shuttle CTM.

Wrap the thread around your hand two times with the bead on the second wrap around your hand. Using the shuttle, tat reversed stitches (not flipped).

Beaded Double Core Reversed Ring (1 - 3 - 2 - 4 - remove the core with the bead on it from your hand and continue 4 - 2 - 4) The last two picots are the bat feet.

Follow the instructions on page 26 to close the BDCRR. The photos in the instructions are for this baby bat. The beaded ring is the body.

First wing

Chain 10 turn

Ring (2 - 2) turn

Chain 10

Tat one reversed DS
shown here on the second wing.

Tat 19 reversed BDS, and then join to the first picot of the body. You will need to push the BDS together so they look like the photo above before doing this join.

Only do the first half of this join then turn the piece over and tighten the threads so that the shuttle thread is on the bottom next to the bat body and the ball thread is on top. Then do the second half of the DS to complete this join.

Chain 4 + This join is to the next picot of the BDCRR. turn

Face

Ring (2 + 4 - 2 - 4) turn

Head outline with ears

Chain 4 + 10 + 1 + 10 + 4 +
The joins before and after the ten DS are to the same picot at the top of the face ring. The chain ten segments are the ears. The last join is to the same picot of the body as the first join of the face ring. It is where the neck joins the body.

Chain 3 - 1 +

Second wing

The second wing is actually a repeat of the first wing. After tatting the second wing tie the ends through the picot of the previous chain. Hide the ends, and then cut them close to the work.

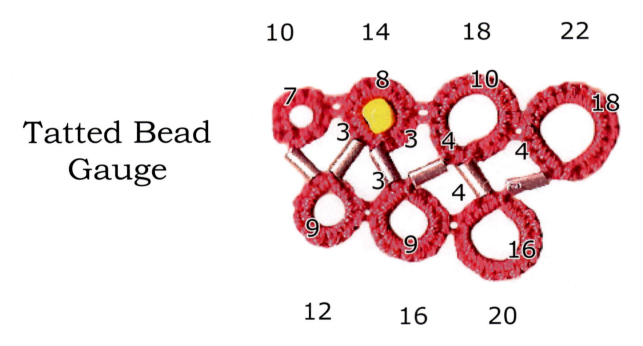

Tatted Bead Gauge

This usefull tool has tube beads between the rings. It helps to determine how many DS to use for any bead. The photo above shows a bead in the middle of the ring with 14 DS.

The ring sizes increment by two. If a bead is too small for one, but too big for the next it should fit perfectly in a ring with the odd number of stitches in between the two.

Bat Games

Make several bats in different colors with a magnetic hematite bead for the body and then use them for some creative play for your little ones of all ages.

Bats in the Belfry

Let the kids cooperatively draw and color scary pictures of a bat cave, or a spooky house. Put the drawings on your refrigerator or some other metal surface with magnets.

The object of the game is to throw the bats at the picture and the winner is the one who has more bats sticking closest to the house or cave.

To make it so that everyone wins, give each child some of every color bats. The winning color is the color to use for icing on cupcakes.

Cupcakes that you just finished making, of course!

Skii Bats

Like skii ball in the arcade.

Use a set of measuring cups in a line, smallest to largest. Each participant must stand behind a line and throw their bats into the measuring cups.

The object is to get the most bats in the smallest measuring cup possible. Even more fun with metal measuring cups if you have them.

So, do bats that stick to the top or the outside of the cups count? Well, maybe they can count as a half a point.

Let the kids determine how many points for each size measuring cup.

Or...

Let the kids decide the object of the games and let them make the rules. Write the rules down and vote on them so that everyone gets a chance to have input.

Children can learn so much from working together, and even when they don't get it all their own way, they learn to co-operate and compromise. Play using one childs choices one time, and another child's choices the next time.

JUST HAVE FUN!

Balanced Double Stitch BDS

There has been some discussion about a sentence from the book, Tatting, by Rhoda Auld published in 1974.

This book contains many inovative ideas which are worthy of note including; combining tatting with macrame and bobbin lace, Zig Zag chains, and adding beads to tatting.

She encouraged tatters to experiment with the tatting techniques and try new ideas. We tatters owe a debt of gratitude to this brilliant lady.

"I formed a ring of double stitches by doubling each half of the knot. This resulted in a solid, chunky ring that looked as though it might contrast well with the ordinary knot. Therefore, I worked a series alternating first one kind of ring and then the other, and joining them together (fig. 6-3e), but, although the new ring took up more space, there was not really enough difference to show."

Auld, Rhoda L. Tatting. New York. Van Nostrand Reinhold Co. 1974. Print. 84-85.

How to tat long chains and large rings that look good.

Tatting, by the mathematical nature of the double stitch, curves around in loops and circles. It does this even if we don't want it to! The field of mathematics called topology actually defines knots in math equations.

OH NO!!! Not math!

I know a number of tatters reading this have just turned green, and then pale. You don't have to be able to do the math to benefit from what it offers. Just like you don't have to understand how a television set works to enjoy watching your favorite shows. Whew!

We can tat loosely and end up with floppy rings and chains that require blocking and stiffening to hold their shape. Or we can have tatting that twists and ruffles and doesn't have a lot of eye appeal. We can design with only smaller rings, and chains that curve, or short chains that will lie nearly straight.

BUT... if we want to tat something with very large rings, or long chains, that is a terrible tatting trouble.

This book includes the Celtic Knot bat that I taught at the Fringe Element tat days two years ago.

There are chains that are 60 stitches that bend in both directions. There are chains over 100 stitches long that curve around just so. I really struggled with the design of this piece, and my first 4 months of attempts were not pretty, and they will never be seen. They went directly into the circular file. Until – Eureka! My husband tied a sliding square knot for me. This is a knot used in rock climbing.

Here is the problem:

The tatting double stitch, pictured here, has the core thread with the knots made around it. Above the core thread there are four cords in the knot. Below the core there are just two. So when the stitches are pushed together there is an angle of about 12 degrees. This can be simply pictured as how the hour and minute hands on a clock look at 2 minutes before noon.

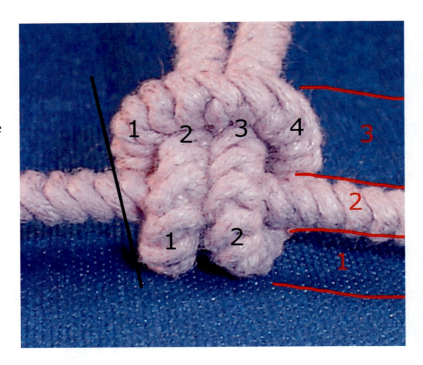

That's not a LOT of difference, unless we take that shape and put many of them side by side: like long tatted chains, and large rings.

 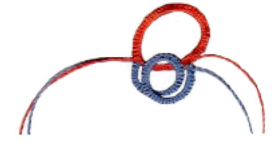 

Fig. A	Fig. B	Fig. C
Ring 35, Chain 35 This looks nice, but notice that the chain curves into about the same shape as the ring.	Ring 60, Chain 60 The ring wants to "ruffle" or twist, and the chain curves around nearly twice. It can be tatted loosely to make it lie flat, but then it is floppy, and must be stiffened and blocked.	This is a ring of 60 stitches tatted with the Balanced Double Stitch Like the long chains in my bat, these stitches hold their shape without blocking or stiffening, and they do not ruffle, or twist.

Here is the solution:

This is a sliding square knot used in rock climbing and ship rigging. Done in tatting, it's a Balanced Double Stitch. There are 4 cords below the core thread, and 4 above, with the extra loops around the core sitting inside the waistband or bump of the stitch. Notice that there is much less of an angle to this knot. It can bend equally up or down.

When many of them are pressed together they can be shaped straight, or in a curve in either direction. No stiffening or blocking is necessary. The ring of 60 BDS, shown in Fig. C on the previous page, is just 60 of this knot tatted tightly. The long chains in the bat are possible using this stitch, whereas with a normal DS, they flipped, and flopped, and twisted all over and ended flopping the bat into the trash can!

How do I tat a BDS? For each half of the balanced double stitch, go around the core thread a second time before tightening the half stitch. Tatting the BDS in needle tatting is easy to do. Just wrap the thread around your finger two times instead of once and then put the tatting needle through the two wraps. Do this for each half of the stitch, and you will have the same effect as shuttle-tatted BDS.

Beaded Double Core Reversed Ring

Put the desired bead on the ball thread before beginning tatting. Start a ring by wrapping the ball thread (NOT the shuttle thread) around your hand two times. Slide the bead onto the second wrap around your hand. Using the shuttle, tat half the required number of RDS, direct tatted stitches, on the two core threads. Remove the core wrap that has the bead on it from your hand, and slide the bead into the middle of the ring.

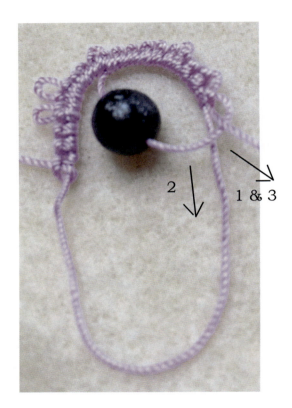

Tat the remaining RDS on the single core thread as shown in the photo at the left

This photo shows half the reversed stitches on the double core loops, and the other half tatted on the core loop that does not have the bead on it. The Beaded core is not quite closed enough yet.

The shuttle thread is on the left, and the core (ball) thread is on the right.

Complete step two, and then pull the core (ball) thread so that the ring closes completely.

The photo on the right shows step three completed.

To close a Beaded Double Core Reversed Ring BDCRR

1.	Pull slightly [about 1"] on the core thread, NOT the shuttle thread!
2.	The core without the bead on it will be a little smaller. Pull on this core thread so the beaded core closes first. Do not close tightly, leave about 1/8" open. When you complete the final step this core will tighten.
3.	Finally, slide the bead up into the middle of the ring and then pull the core thread until the ring is completely closed around the bead.

Made in the USA
Monee, IL
17 September 2021